YOUR FRIENDS & NEIGHBORS
NEIGHBORS
Neil LaBute

ff

faber and faber

First published in 1998
by Faber and Faber Limited
3 Queen Square London WC1N 3AU

Photoset by Parker Typesetting Service, Leicester
Printed in England by Clays Ltd, St Ives plc

© Polygram Filmed Entertainment, 1998

Photographs by Bruce Birmelin © 1998 Gramercy Pictures

Neil LaBute is hereby identified as
author of this work in accordance with Section 77 of the
Copyright, Designs and Patents Act 1988

A CIP record for this book
is available from the British Library

ISBN 0-571-19791-4

2 4 6 8 10 9 7 5 3 1

CONTENTS

INTRODUCTION
Some Thoughts on Creation

Looking back over this manuscript, it's amusing to see how a piece of writing evolves. My first impulse for this screenplay was to call it *Lepers*, as I felt that it dealt with a particular social disease of the nineties – our inability/unwillingness to connect and our rabid desire to serve our own interests at any cost. During pre-production on the film, however, *Lepers* was largely seen as marketing death (a part of the business I am only now begrudgingly trying to comprehend) and the search was on for an equally fitting but palatable title. Jason Patric and I became fixated on the idea of using the George Harrison song 'I Me Mine', as it seemed both evocative on its own and quite indicative of the screenplay's main themes. *I Me Mine* suggests a world well beyond the 'me generation', mutated to a place that might best be described as the 'me me me generation'. Mr Harrison's song spoke loudly to both Jason and Myself; unfortunately, so did the difficulties of licencing a Beatles song. On we continued. *Your Friends & Neighbors* came about because of its obvious innocuous charm and the vague sense of indictment that it brings to each viewer and/or reader. Whether you like it or not, you know the type of people who populate the film and these pages – they are your friends and neighbors. Not all of them, to be sure, but representative enough to be frighteningly and hilariously real. Like the Restoration playwrights I so admire, I love the idea of criticizing my audience as I entertain them. One must be cruel to be kind.

Ideas get lost, priorities shift, the magic of editing takes over and you find your movie almost by default in the end. This film is not a documentary, it doesn't attempt to speak for a generation or even a section therein. It merely shines a light on a small set of characters who do exist out there today, a collection of mindsets that are valid simply because they are actively functioning among us. Above all, I hope *Your Friends & Neighbors* is a dramatic entertainment that still has the courage to instruct and a willingness to be truer to its story and characters than an audience's expectations. Writing is my 'new math'. I try to set up a series of rules and obstacles for myself, then follow them through to their conclusion while all the time pushing boundaries. Logical but never predictable, good writing should be as unexpected for the writer as it is for the reader. Know where you're going but not exactly how to get there. And so it is with *Your Friends & Neighbors* – unexpected, troublesome, the bastard child of some themes and a title now altered and pounded into submission.

Thematically, I've lately been accused of graduating (with honors, I trust) from Misogyny to Misanthropy, but I find myself a hopeful realist; as Edward Bond once said, almost 'irresponsibly optimistic'. My approach is a bit clinical, my outlook often troubled, but my hopes for us all are largely untarnished. This script represents life as it easily can be lived if one is not careful, so proceed with caution. This is not a race. Your mileage may vary.

NEIL LABUTE

Producer Jason Patric and Aaron Eckhart discuss a scene with
writer/director Neil LaBute

The cast and crew of *Your Friends & Neighbors* is as follows:

MARY	Amy Brenneman
BARRY	Aaron Eckhart
TERRI	Catherine Keener
CHERI	Nastassja Kinski
CARY	Jason Patric
JERRY	Ben Stiller

Casting	Mali Finn, C.S.A.
Costume Designer	April Napier
Editor	Joel Plotch
Production Designer	Charles Breen
Director of Photography	Nancy Schreiber, A.S.C.
Co-Producer	Philip Steuer
Executive Producers	Alix Madigan-Yorkin
	Stephen Pevner
Produced by	Steve Golin
	Jason Patric
Written and Directed by	Neil LaBute

A Propaganda Films/Fleece production
A Gramercy Pictures presentation
Gramercy Pictures is a Polygram company

Your Friends & Neighbors

SILENCE. DARKNESS.

INT. STUDIO – NIGHT

A sleek, modern room nearly erupting with African art. Statues in various corners. Paintings on the walls. Beneath a skylight sits A RAISED BEDSTAND *all drenched in black bed dressings. Pillows. Sheets. Everything. Like a Herb Ritts video, only worse.*

Beneath the pile somewhere lies CARY, *handsome, compact, thirties, pumping away for all he's worth.*

He moves at a brisk pace, forcing the mattress to shudder markedly beneath his chiseled weight. He studies HIS PARTNER *as he moves.*

> CARY
> I mean, is it me? Because I think you're a great lay . . . no, I mean that. I feel . . . special . . . coming inside you. I'm serious. I'm always gonna think of you as a very special fuck . . . and I only hope that you like it.

A burst of concentrated energy takes his breath away and he speaks in gasps.

> Ohh . . . that's good. Is it . . . not something? What? Not tender? Should I be being more tender now . . . or add some sweetness?

THE BODY MOTION *stops cold as Cary nearly springs out of bed, whipping the covers out of his way. Only now is it obvious that there is no one beneath him. He is fully clothed from the waist down; he glances at his watch and smiles. Suddenly he picks up a small tape recorder from the nightstand and rewinds it. He presses* PLAY *and listens to himself in the act. He smiles.*

> Yeah, I'd believe that . . . I mean, if I was a chick I'd believe it . . .
>
> *(resets the recorder)*

3

Alright. One more time before she gets here . . . come on, let's pick up the pace.

The watch gets a second glance, then Cary is back at it, thrusting and jabbing through another practice round for all he's worth.

BLACKOUT. BLAST OF CREDITS.

SLOW FADE IN ON:

INT. THE THEATRE – DAY

An industrial space with dark maroon seating. A SEMI-CIRCLE *of* INDIVIDUALS *listen to Jerry, a tall man in his mid-thirties, as he rehearses a scene from Wycherley's* The Country Wife *with* AN ATTRACTIVE YOUNG CO-ED.

> JERRY
> (*in character voice*)
> 'Gad, though you laugh now, 'twill be my turn 'ere long! Oh women, more impertinent, more cunning, and more mischievous than their monkeys, and to me almost as ugly. She has been throwing me about, and rifling all I have . . .
> (*throws her to the bed*)
> But I'll get in to her the back way, and so rifle her for it!'
> (*breaks character*)
> Scene . . .

Jerry drops his hands and takes a deep breath and an acting moment, CHUCKLING *a bit as* HIS STUDENTS MURMUR *to themselves until Jerry quiets them.*

Okay, alright, now I know your classmate and I've turned this into a provocative little scene, I know that, but that is always the challenge, even in a period piece. I mean, what're we looking at here? Huh? Lace and language aside, in the end it's just men and women, right? Just like any other story, like every story, and ultimately, what do these characters want? Hmm? I know, it's embarrassing for you to say, but . . . let's be honest, they wanna fuck! Correct? It's always all about fucking . . .

4

A RELEASE OF LAUGHTER *from the students.* ONE CO-ED *smiles up from beneath her trendy rimless glasses. Jerry returns it.*

CUT TO:

INT. APARTMENT – NIGHT

Handsomely decorated but cramped apartment. Bookcases line the four walls. Framed posters of dead foreign authors abound.

A BEAUTIFUL BED *is shaking wildly as* A COUPLE *performs furiously in the darkness. Impossible to make them out clearly but the rhythm is undeniable. Almost catchy. Like Billie Holiday taking on the horn section in the back of a bus.*

JERRY *is crouched behind* TERRI, *a striking woman in her early thirties. He attacks her with zeal as they go, cloaked only by a thin sheet.*

>   JERRY
> Oh yeah . . . yeah, that's it. Oh yeah, I'm with you. Baby!
> Absolutely. Can you feel it? That's right. You and I are in
> complete . . . harmony . . . here. Mmm . . .

TERRI *stops cold but Jerry continues his 'erotic' monologue as he drives along.*

>   TERRI
> Is there any chance you're gonna shut the fuck up?

>   JERRY
> What?

JERRY *stiffens and stops, taking a moment to collect his thoughts and catch his breath. Terri moves away and snaps on a lamp.*

>   TERRI
> You're talking right in my ear. I'm losing any sense of
> concentration that I might've had.

>   JERRY
> Well . . . I'm just . . . it's kinda hard to stop in the . . .

>   TERRI
> Well, keep it to yourself. I mean, 'Can you feel it?' Your thing

is nearly in the back of my throat! You think I'm gonna miss that?
> (*beat*)

Let's just do it, I don't need the narration. Okay?

JERRY *is still kneeling but quickly moves away from his partner and settles down into the blankets for the battle.*

> JERRY

What is this?

> TERRI

I'm sorry, but this is not a travelogue, you know?

> JERRY

Jesus.

> TERRI

It's how I feel . . .

> JERRY

Oh, great. That's great . . .

Jerry gets up and starts getting dressed.

> TERRI

Why do we always have to go through this shit?
> (*beat*)

I've always been that way.

> JERRY

Yeah, I know, and it's so fucking . . . enjoyable, you know? I mean, I so much as start to breathe, and you stop! What is that?

> TERRI

It's me.

> JERRY

Yeah, well, it's fucked!

> TERRI

Okay.
> (*sighs*)

. . . you wanna watch TV?

6

JERRY

No, I don't wanna watch . . . Why is it that your cunt is like –
and I don't like to use that word, but goddammit! – it's like
your vagina is seemingly tied directly to my mouth? Why is
that? Huh?! It's like, I so much as crack open my lips for a
breath and you're squeezing me off . . . What is that? It's like
our two organs are on some fucking pullcord here and I'm
. . . I'm . . . You know what I'm sick of it!!

(*beat*)

I'll talk as much as I like!

TERRI

Good. I hope she enjoys it . . . 'cause you won't be fucking
me.

JERRY

Fine. That's beautiful. That's lovely . . .

Jerry is dressed now and he grabs his jacket from a chair.

Could I have my keys, please?

Terri, back on the bed, scoops them off a nightstand and holds them up,
JINGLING *them provocatively while Jerry, in no mood, holds his hand
out impatiently. Terri begins to smile and shake her head 'No' when
Jerry* SNAPS *his fingers. Her smile freezes over and she tosses the keys at
him a bit hard. They catch his finger and glance off on to the floor. He*
CURSES HER QUIETLY *and sucks on his hand as he retrieves the ring.*

TERRI

Where you going?

JERRY

I don't know . . . out! I feel like talking . . . I just wanna chat!!
Okay?

TERRI

Look, we can talk . . . I just don't want something in my ass
while we're doing it.

JERRY

Go fuck yourself.

TERRI

Don't give me any ideas. Hey!

JERRY

What!

TERRI

Hey . . . bring me some ice cream if you go by a store.
Okay? . . .

THE DOOR *swings open and Jerry stands in the archway, glaring at her. After a moment, he* SLAMS *it for effect as he exits.*

SUDDENLY ALONE *for a moment, Terri reaches across for the television remote. She pulls the sheet over herself and leans back.*

CUT TO:

INT. OFFICE – DAY

A simple, handsome space with a wooden desk at one end. Glass on several sides, allowing for a view of towering buildings in the distance. Barry, a plain-looking, muscular man of about thirty-five, sits back in a swivel chair, chewing down a sandwich and TALKING *while* AN ASSOCIATE *sits opposite him, digging into a meatball sub. Both in regulation shirt, tie, suspenders. The works.*

BARRY

. . . So you want to know . . . what? The 'best' lay I've ever
had? Right?

A PIECE OF SANDWICH *slips from his sagging hoagie to the desk as both men guffaw at this notion. Barry reaches over and rescues the fallen meat from his blotter, gobbling it up as he smiles over at his co-worker.*

That's easy . . . It's me. Nobody gives me more pleasure than
I give myself. I mean that. I mean, not that my wife's terrible
or anything . . . she's not, she's wonderful . . . but she's just
not . . . me. You know? And I like doing it with her, I do . . .
but I'll tell you, the real fireworks take place when she heads
off to the shower . . . know what I mean?

8

THE MEN *share* ANOTHER GOOD-NATURED LAUGH *at Barry's hand gestures while they munch away.*

You probably think I'm kidding, but I've lived with this . . . hell . . . all my life and I'm telling you, nobody makes me come the way I do.

CUT TO:

INT. BROWNSTONE BEDROOM – NIGHT

A master bedroom in a newly restored brownstone. Moving boxes stacked in corners. Designer sheets cover the windows. Martha Stewart in the making. In the middle of the room sits AN ENORMOUS BED *covered in mounds of stark white sheets.* TWO FIGURES *are struggling in the sea of fabric, pushing against each other. Making love but distant.*

MARY, a quiet, pretty woman in her early thirties, lies on her side and clutches a pillow as BARRY *holds himself up on one elbow and looks over at his wife as he works. She opens her mouth to speak but catches herself. Her husband shifts forward, glancing at the time and briefly ending the siege.*

BARRY
Hmm? Oh yeah. Yeah. Come on . . . Come on . . .

There is only silence from Mary as he quietly disengages.

I'm sorry. I just . . . I mean . . . Oh God . . . Is it me? I need to . . . I just got a bad go of it from here . . . that's all. Your legs don't open as cleanly from . . . I mean, is this something you really like? This 'side-saddle' thing? Hmm?

BARRY *shifts his weight about, propping himself up with an armload of pillows. He's digging in for a long campaign.*

You feel it's me, don't you? I can just . . .
(*beat*)
Hey, honey, I'll bet Adam and Eve, you know, from the Old Testament . . . they probably never did it on their side. I mean, until they were out of the garden, like after they were thrown out . . . or bored. Or something.

9

A SMILE *appears on his lips at this thought but quickly fades.*

> Because it's just not a natural . . . It's me, isn't it? Of course it is, or you'd be talking.
> > (*beat*)
>
> We could just start again . . . honey? Because I'm still quite hard. Really. It's completely firmed up. Down there. Seriously, we could just . . .

Without turning, Mary finally speaks.

> MARY
> Shh, shhh. Please. Please be quiet.

Silence. After a moment, Barry rolls over on his side, away from his wife. He begins masturbating.

CUT TO:

INT. BROWNSTONE LIVING ROOM. LATER THAT SUMMER – DAY

A cozy living room still under construction. Picture frames and opened cartons pushed against the walls. Drinks are scattered about the floor and a stereo PLAYS JAZZ *somewhere in the distance.* BARRY AND MARY *have invited Jerry and Terri for dinner.*

> TERRI
> I mean, could you guys be any happier?

> MARY
> . . . no.

> TERRI
> I mean it . . . look at this!

> BARRY
> Oh, no, no . . . you kidding?

> MARY
> No, this is, this place is . . .

> BARRY
> It's heaven. Really, it is. It's a dream house.

                              JERRY

This is the one, huh?

                              BARRY

Absolutely, no question.
                             (*beat*)
I could see us here twenty years, easy.

                              TERRI

Wow. Yeah, I would love a spot like this . . .

Terri nods. Mary kisses Barry on the cheek.

                              JERRY

Hmm. Interesting.

CUT TO:

INT. BROWNSTONE DINING ROOM. LATER — DAY

                              BARRY
                   (*sets a gift in front of Mary*)
For the lady of the house.

                              MARY
                          (*surprised*)
No . . . I thought we decided not to . . .

                              BARRY

It's nothing. It's Okay . . .

                              JERRY

Is it your birthday? Am I missing . . .?

                              MARY

No. He just likes to spoil me.

                              JERRY

Well, good man.

Mary opens it.

                              MARY

Ohh . . . honey. A watch?
                  (*winding it and holding it to her ear*)

BARRY

No, you're not supposed to do that.

TERRI

An antique, too. Oh, it's beautiful.

JERRY

It's broken. Isn't it?

BARRY

No, it's . . .

MARY

That's Okay.
(*examining it*)
Because it's still . . . very . . .

BARRY

It's a bracelet. You see . . .
(*takes it*)
I mean, yes, it's stopped, and all, but it's meant. It's just for show. You wear it as jewelry, you know? Haven't you ever seen that?

MARY

Ummm . . . that's so sweet.

TERRI

Yeah, I've seen that. You just wear it.

JERRY

You have?

TERRI

Huh?
(*beat*)
So, what's your point?

JERRY

Look, I'm not trying to be, you know, but just because it's not working . . . I mean, their motive behind having it on? That day. Or whenever. How could you possibly, just in passing, know that? That's all I'm saying. Forget it. It's just . . .

13

Long pause.

BARRY

They're quite big in Europe . . .

TERRI

You'd know.

MARY

Anyhow, it's beautiful . . .

TERRI

Of course, you'd know.

MARY
(*a peck to Barry's cheek*)
I'm sorry I didn't get you anything.

BARRY

Oh, no problem.

JERRY

I'm . . . look . . . I'm just . . . I was just . . . Forget it, alright?

TERRI

Why would you wear around a watch that doesn't work?!
(*to Barry*)
I mean, unless you meant to . . . like this one? I mean, why
would you do that?

JERRY

Let's just forget it.
(*beat*)
I was just trying to, you know . . .

TERRI

I do not get you . . . always with the goddamn semiotics. I
mean, it's a gift, it's not fucking *Medea*. Can it please just be
what it is?! It's a bracelet! Shit . . .
(*beat*)
Sorry . . . is that gold?

BARRY

. . . yeah. Plate, I think . . .

TERRI

Huh.

CUT TO:

INT. BROWNSTONE LIVING ROOM. EVEN LATER – DAY

Huge windows line one wall and soft furniture is pushed about at angles. Jerry, Terri and Mary are seated, the debris of their meal in front of them.

Barry is standing, licking the last of some sauce from his plate with the edge of a croissant.

BARRY

We really don't do this enough, do we?

JERRY

No, we don't.

Barry leaves.

MARY

Do you guys want some more wine to go with . . .

Terri finishes her glass, holding it out expectantly toward Jerry.

TERRI

Yeah. I opened that other bottle in the kitchen.
(*looks over at Jerry*)
I guess I'll get it.

TERRI *gathers up an armful of glasses, accidentally spilling a drop or two on one sleeve of Jerry's jacket. He reacts violently.*

JERRY

Hey, hey, watch it! Geez. This is doe-skin, remember?

TERRI

Yeah.
(*to herself*)
I bought it for you, remember.

A CHUCKLE *from Mary stirs Jerry to pursue the issue.*

JERRY

What?!

TERRI

Nothing . . .

AN INNOCENT SMILE. *She exits without waiting for an answer.*
DISHES *are picked at self-consciously as Jerry and Mary find themselves
left alone in the room.*

JERRY

Jesus, this stuff really stains.

*Mary gets up and sits beside Terry on the couch and blots the stain for
him with a napkin.*

MARY

Yeah, but don't rub it in like that. You just kind of blot it.
That's better.

JERRY

Thanks. This place is really great.

MARY

Thanks.
(*beat*)
I can't believe it was May that we, you know . . .

JERRY

Yeah . . . yeah.

MARY

We really loved seeing you in that play. That was . . .

JERRY

Oh, thank you . . . right.

MARY

Yeah, I don't know how you guys do that! You know, getting
up in front of people and . . .

JERRY

Well, Shakespeare's a gift, really.

MARY

Hmm . . .

Jerry nods as an uncomfortable silence settles in. Mary fiddles with her new bracelet.

So . . . how're things?

JERRY

Good. You?

MARY

Oh, you know . . . we're fine.

JERRY

Great. Us too.

JERRY'S EYES *study her a moment with genuine interest. After a moment, she blushes and turns away, absently running a hand through her hair.*

PLATES CLATTERING *in the kitchen and* WARM CHATTER *catches Jerry's attention briefly. He weighs the odds and decides to risk it.*

Listen, I need to ask you something.

MARY

Hmm?

JERRY

Can I call you? Could we get together sometime?

MARY

What? I mean . . . you want . . . ?

JERRY

Whenever. You tell me. I want to . . . if you pick a time, or place . . . I'll be there. Or call me. Uhh, just . . . can we?

MARY *studies him closely for a minute while he glances down the hallway in the direction of the kitchen.*

BARRY'S FAINT LAUGH *can be heard as he* RUMMAGES *through various kitchen drawers.*

In the kitchen – same time. Barry carries desserts as Terri is getting the spoons from a drawer.

TERRI

Should I set these? The big ones?

BARRY

Yeah. Yeah. Get the big ones.

TERRI

For the mousse. So what should I do with these. Do I just put them as garnish on top?

BARRY

Yeah, put 'em on. Put it in here. Make little . . .

Back in the main room.

JERRY
(*whispering*)

I'd like to get together with you.

MARY

Oh. For . . .?

HER FRAGILE FINGERS *are carefully scooped up in Jerry's hands.*

JERRY

I mean, we could talk. I mean, talking would actually be nice, also. I just . . .
(*beat*)

MARY

This is . . .

JERRY

I know.

MARY

I mean.

JERRY

If I have to wait another year to see you and chat over cherry, what, mousse?

MARY

(*overlapping*)

. . . mousse.

JERRY

I just don't . . . you tell me. I know I'm taking a chance here.

JERRY *straightens and moves away seconds before the dessert and wine arrive in the eager hands of Barry and Terri. Barry dips an index finger in the dark red sauce and sucks on it for emphasis.*

BARRY

Sorry we took so long.

JERRY

No problem.

TERRI

We got to talking and we couldn't shut up.

Terri smiles and starts handing out glasses. Jerry gets one as well as Barry moves past him, a big smile plastered across his face.

JERRY

Look at this. This is like . . . You made this?

BARRY

Ohh, you're not gonna believe what this woman can do with a cherry!

MARY *gets a quick nuzzle from Barry as he sits. Jerry smiles weakly at Barry, then steals a glance at Mary. She eats her meal, head down, in silence.*

CUT TO:

INT. BROWNSTONE FOYER. LATER STILL – DAY

A warmly tiled entryway. Ficus trees guard a massive door that holds back the street. Terri kisses Mary, then Barry as she and Jerry prepare to leave.

JERRY

Thank you.

                              TERRI
Thank you. What a great day.

                              BARRY
Yeah. It was fun.

A BRIGHT LIGHT *floods the room as Barry opens the door, allowing the late afternoon sun to spill in as they all hug. They all turn away from the harsh blast of day. Jerry follows Mary with his eyes as she starts upstairs, then follows Terri and Barry out the door. He looks about, desperate for a smokescreen.*

Lemme walk you to the corner.

                              JERRY
You know what? I'm gonna . . . I'm gonna use the bathroom.

                              BARRY
You remember where it is?

                              JERRY
Yeah, yeah, yeah . . .

                              TERRI
Don't splosh. Remember? It's porcelain.

                              JERRY
Right. Thank you. Okay, go ahead. I'll see you guys out there.

Barry follows Terri out the door as JERRY *hurries down a hallway that leads to a landing as the front door closes. He cocks his head, listening for a moment, then dashes upstairs.*

INT. MASTER BEDROOM – DAY

Mary sits on the far side of the huge bedroom, lost on the mattress. Jerry enters the room and moves to her, breathless, and kneels down.

                              JERRY
May tenth. That's the last time I saw you. On the pier. I remember it exactly. I remember the date. Time . . .

                              MARY
You remember the . . .?

JERRY

You were wearing a red skirt –

MARY

– and a white . . .

JERRY

. . . blouse. And you were such a knockout . . .

MARY

I'm just . . . so . . .

(*weakly*)

Why are you doing this?

JERRY

Because I'm . . . I'm just . . . Tell me that you've thought
about me. Because I can't stop thinking about you. I wanna
hold you.

MARY

I've thought about you.

CUT TO:

INT. BROWNSTONE FOYER. SAME TIME – DAY

*Mary and Jerry come slowly down the stairs, not talking yet saying
volumes. Mary turns slowly to face Jerry, a thin book from a nearby
stack on an antiquated table in her hands. She hurriedly opens a drawer
and pulls out a pen. She scribbles down a number and a short message,
kisses it and closes the cover.*

MARY

Call me tomorrow . . .

*They smile at one another as Jerry clutches the volume in one hand,
breathing in the fragrance of the paper.*

*Terri enters through the doorway. She takes them both in with a
glowing smile.*

TERRI

Hey, are you ready?

JERRY

Hey. Just coming.

Jerry nervously clutches the dust jacket of his secret. THE BOOK *is held up by Jerry for Terri's disinterested inspection in the ensuing silence.*

I borrowed a book. Camus.

TERRI

Oh. Great. Perfect. It'll really set off the rest.
(*to Mary*)
Do you have bookshelves in your bathroom? I'm lucky enough to.

JERRY

Ha-ha-ha.

THE WOMEN LAUGH *as Terri heads back through the door, Jerry a step behind her. Terri hugs and kisses Mary.*

TERRI

God, you know, it was great to see you guys again. We should do something . . . just, you know, you and me. We always say that, but . . .

MARY

That'd be great. Later this week.

TERRI

Really? Lunch maybe. Great. We should get together more often than this.

MARY

Right. I can't believe it was May the last time.

JERRY

God, that's unbelievable.

Jerry kisses Mary.

See ya.

TERRI

Bye.

Bye.

Terri smiles at Jerry and takes his hand, leading him toward the door. As he walks, he steals a quick look back at Mary. She has already turned away.

CUT TO:

INT. HEALTH CLUB TRACK. ANOTHER AFTERNOON – DAY

Cary and Barry jog down a wooden path, bathed in sweat. They dance in and out of pools of daylight and shadow as they move past windows, a basketball court, etc. The place is nearly empty.

CARY

Three minutes. I need to cool down. It's actually a shitty place to run. I mean, it's a nice old gym, it's quiet, but there's no girls around. That's why we can't get him in here during the week.

BARRY

I left a message.

CARY

Fuck. He's busy.

BARRY

Right.

CARY

Papers to grade. What a life . . .

BARRY

True . . . anyway, he's the smart one. It's humid today!

CARY

No shit. Fucking boiling, even with that A/C on . . . You sweat your dick off, have a heart attack . . . PHEWW!

BARRY

Do you wanna meet later, go downtown?

CARY

Why? We just ran.

24

BARRY

No, I'm saying, I got that corporate membership.

CARY

So?

BARRY

Well, I could get you in.

CARY

Hey, I don't need anybody to 'get me in', especially with those office assholes downtown at lunchtime. No offense.
(*beat*)
Hate that . . .

BARRY

That's not what I'm saying. I'm saying there's a lot of women there. That's all.

CARY

So? What, are you expecting me to change my routine for those people? Fat chance. If the ladies want to see us, they'll quit their designer workout bullshit and they'll drag their fat cans over here and run. Okay? 'Cause even though I personally think this is a fucked place to exercise, I do it. To spite 'em.

                    BARRY
Who?

                    CARY
Everybody.

CUT TO:

INT. ART GALLERY. SAME TIME – DAY

Terri stands in front of the oversized canvas and stares up at it. A FEW PATRONS mill past. The new exhibit is still on the floor, waiting to be hung. After a moment.

CHERI *approaches Terri and they both stand in silence, looking up at the mammoth unframed work.*

                    CHERI
Hi.

                    TERRI
How're you?

                    CHERI
Fine, thanks.

                    TERRI
Great . . .

SILENCE *for another second. Cheri starts to move off as Terri stops her with a question.*

Do you know, is this part of a collection, or is it . . .

                    CHERI
No, it's just a single piece. Nice, isn't it?

                    TERRI
Very.

                    CHERI
First time here?

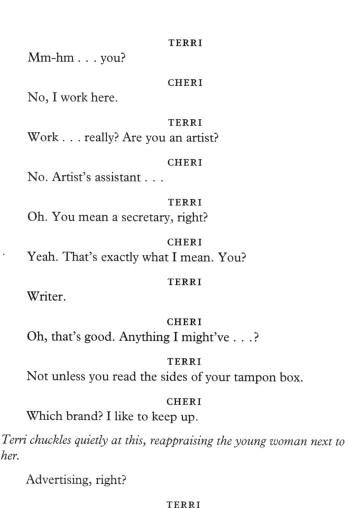

TERRI

Mm-hm . . . you?

CHERI

No, I work here.

TERRI

Work . . . really? Are you an artist?

CHERI

No. Artist's assistant . . .

TERRI

Oh. You mean a secretary, right?

CHERI

Yeah. That's exactly what I mean. You?

TERRI

Writer.

CHERI

Oh, that's good. Anything I might've . . .?

TERRI

Not unless you read the sides of your tampon box.

CHERI

Which brand? I like to keep up.

Terri chuckles quietly at this, reappraising the young woman next to her.

Advertising, right?

TERRI

Yeah.

CHERI

That's great . . .

TERRI

Especially if you're a tampon.

CHERI

No. It's nice to be good at anything.

TERRI

Well, who said I was good?

CHERI

I'm guessing.

TERRI

This really is a lovely piece.

CHERI

Yeah. It is.

TERRI

Can I buy you lunch?

CUT TO:

INT. BROWNSTONE BEDROOM. A DIFFERENT EVENING – NIGHT

Mary sits on the bed speaking in WHISPERS *into the phone. Barry is* WHISTLING *just out of sight in the bathroom.*

BARRY

Honey, should I go with the, what's this called, 'loden', or the . . .?

MARY

Yeah . . . no, no. The salmon, I think.
(back to Jerry)
Yeah, he's right here. No, I mean, in the house. No, I don't want to put him on. Please . . . stop it.

THE WHISTLING STOPS *and the bathroom door begins to swing open. Mary finishes in a hurry.*

I have to go. He's coming. Yeah, Okay. Yeah. It's good talking to you too. Alright. Bye-bye.

BARE-CHESTED *and smiling curiously, Barry enters the room as she hangs up.*

BARRY

Who was that?

28

MARY

Your best friend.

BARRY

What? I just spoke with him twenty minutes ago. He didn't
want to talk to me?

MARY

Uh-uh . . .

A SHIRT *is pulled from a wardrobe shelf by Barry but he doesn't put it
on yet. He crosses to the bed and sits.*

BARRY

I told him I'd be there. He knows I'll be there. I'm the one
who invited him.

A SHRUG *from Mary puts the conversation on hold. Barry edges toward
her, his shirt held in one hand. Slowly he begins to kiss her neck.*

CUT TO:

INT. SPORTS BAR. LATER ON – NIGHT

*Cavernous space, but nearly empty tonight. Barry sits across from Cary
in a booth.*

CARY
(*studying Barry's shirt*)

What is that, pink?

BARRY

This? No, it's salmon . . .

CARY

You might think about puttin' that jacket back on.

BARRY

Why?

CARY

Where'd you get it?

BARRY

My wife gave it to me.

CARY

Hm. Enough said . . .
                    (*looking about again*)
It's past eleven. Where the fuck is everybody!

BARRY

Hmm. Anyway, so how'd this thing turn out? Did she say
she'd made a mistake or . . .?

CARY

Huh? Oh, no, that . . . nah, I fucked her. Complete revenge
fuck, which are always the best.

BARRY

Really? You . . . I mean . . .

CARY

I don't kid about shit like that. See, she had questioned a
decision I'd made at work, so, you know, I had to.

BARRY

Sure.

CARY

Anyway, I wine her a little, dine her a touch . . . get her back
to my place. So, we're in bed . . .

INT. SPORTS BAR PHONE NOOK. SAME TIME – NIGHT

*Jerry stands at a pay phone, receiver in one hand. He plays with a
handful of change as he* WHISPERS *into the mouthpiece.*

JERRY

I know . . . This just seemed like a good time, I wanted to call
back. No, he's over on the other side of the room. Yeah,
that'd be fine. Yes, I'll be there. It was my idea, of course I'll
be there. What do you have on? No . . . I don't mean the
music. What're you wearing?

INT. SPORTS BAR. SAME TIME – NIGHT

*Cary and Barry still talking in their distant corner. Barry checks his
watch and glances back at Cary.*

30

I slip my cock out, right, I mean, completely jerk it right out. And I turn her back over – kinda rough, by her hair – and I tell her to get the fuck out of my place. And if she ever does that to a guy again – you know, crosses one of us in public like that – I'll fuckin' kill her. And I think she believed me.

BARRY *has long since stopped nursing his gin and sits with his mouth wide open.*

BARRY

Jesus . . . you're not making this up.

CARY

Fuck no. This happened. You know? I am not one to be messed with. I don't give a shit about anybody. This is my life.

JERRY *returns to the table without any refreshments. Cary spots this in a second.*

JERRY

Oh, shit . . . Do you want me to go . . .?

CARY

No.

(*beat*)

Anyway, I got a letter in the mail. This was a couple of weeks ago. Full apology. She even had one put in my personnel file. Huh? It's no big thing, but it was enough to let me know I was justified in what I did.

BARRY

Man . . .

JERRY

So . . . what do you guys wanna do tonight?

BARRY

Has he told you this story?

JERRY

No, but I'm sure it's great.

CARY

Yeah? How would you know?

BARRY

It's incredible . . .

CARY

You'd have taken the same steps. Common decency dictated the whole thing.

THE MEN *have a* GOOD-NATURED *laugh at this one, continuing to drink as they survey their options.*

CUT TO:

INT. LOFT. SAME TIME – NIGHT

Inside Cheri's place. The city spread wide and twinkling through ceiling-high windows. Pillows and artwork dominate the room. A futon tossed in one corner. Cheri and Terri sit comfortably on the floor, sipping wine and staring off into the night.

TERRI

Oh, who cares? It's a sickness, anyway.

CHERI

What is?

TERRI

All of it. Relationships. Caring. Love's a disease. You know, it really is.

CHERI

Yeah, but it's curable.

TERRI

Hmmm.

(*smiling*)

Who said that again?

CHERI

I don't remember her name. It's true, though, isn't it?

TERRI

Oh yeah.

Silence.

CHERI

I'm glad you called . . .

TERRI

I'm glad you were home.

A KISS *suddenly erupts between the two women. Nothing tentative. Just long and wet.*

CUT TO:

INT. BOOK STORE. SAME TIME – DAY

Little 'Ma & Pa' place downtown. Walls bursting with books, mounds of trinkets, etc. Not a customer in sight except for Barry and Jerry standing in one aisle, TALKING *leisurely while Jerry browses through a stack of vintage paperbacks.*

JERRY

I have no idea what happened. I mean, something happened. Obviously. Some 'thing' happened and I don't know what it was. She turned on me.

BARRY

Come on . . .

JERRY

She says I talk. Okay? I'm a talker. I'm accused of speaking. I
mean, we're screwing, for Christ's sake! It's like 'screwing',
you know, like in 'screwing around'! There's supposed to be a
degree of improvisation, isn't there? Jesus . . .

THE FRIENDS *glance at one another knowingly as Barry fiddles with a
boxed set.*

So now I don't speak, I hold my breath . . . I make love like
we're in some nursing home. Know what? She laughs in my
face.

BARRY

Man . . . I don't know what to . . . you're staying together?
Right?

JERRY

I dunno . . . I suppose. I mean, we split the rent. We bought
a TV. This huge fucking bed. I mean, we have investments in
this. And I still have feeling there.

                    BARRY
Hmm . . .

                    JERRY
Hey listen, thanks for the ear. You guys just go have a good
time.

                    BARRY
I really appreciate that tip. It sounds like a great place.

                    JERRY
Yeah, it's nice.

                    BARRY
Kinda romantic.

                    JERRY
Uh-huh. Hey, say 'Hi' to the wife for me, would ya?

                    BARRY
Sure.

CUT TO:

INT. COFFEE SHOP. SAME TIME – DAY

Terri's hangout. Quiet, especially at lunchtime. ONLY A FEW
CUSTOMERS *and* EMPLOYEES *mill about or sit eating.*

TERRI AND MARY *share a table as they devour enormous salads. Terri
smiles over at Mary, who self-consciously glances over from time to time.*

                    MARY
Why would I even categorize something as 'the best' . . . well,
you know, that I've had? That's just . . . absurd.

                    TERRI
Okay, Okay . . .

                    MARY
No, I just . . . do not store up little sexual tidbits on . . . No.
Not at all.

                    TERRI
Really?

MARY

Come on . . . Even though I probably should. It'd make a good freelance piece, but I don't . . .
(*beat*)
I mean, not that there hasn't been a good one . . . or two. Or that I haven't had a best . . . 'fuck' – I hate that word, anyway – or anything like that. I have. I'm sure I have. I just have to reach back. That's all. Call it up.

A SIP *of wine gives her courage as she toys with the memories.*

CUT TO:

INT. ART GALLERY. SAME TIME – DAY

Cary stands looking up at a huge canvas overhead. Cheri moves toward him, speaking warmly.

CHERI

Hi.

CARY

How're you?

CHERI

Fine, thanks.

CARY

Great.
(*beat*)
Do you know, is this part of a collection, or is it, umm . . .?

CHERI

No, it's just a single piece. Nice, isn't it?

CARY

Very.

CHERI

First time here?

CARY

Uh-huh. You?

36

CHERI

No, I work here.

CARY

Work . . . really? You're an artist.

CHERI

No. Artist's assistant.

CARY

That's terrific. Listen . . . I'm gonna be open with you. I spotted you outside. You're really great-looking. Maybe we could get a drink or something. What time are you off? I bet you're tremendous in bed . . .

Cheri abruptly turns heel and walks away to help ANOTHER CUSTOMER. *Unfazed, Cary turns back to the painting and continues to study as he* YAWNS LOUDLY.

Who is she kidding? . . .
(*to himself*)
'Artist's assistant'?

CUT TO:

37

A modern chain-store shoved into the bottom of a high-rise. A FEW
SHOPPERS *and store* CREW MEMBERS *bustling about in their shiny red
vests. Barry and Mary moving down the aisles with a purpose. Mary
pushes a basket forward with determination while Barry catches up with
some Ban roll-on.*

> BARRY
>
> I just think we really need to keep trying, you know? I know
> it's me and all, but . . . we gotta keep at it. You know that we
> are gonna open some floodgates here.

The cart comes to an abrupt halt and Mary looks at her husband,
SPEAKING *in hushed but deliberate tones.*

> MARY
>
> I know what you're saying, but . . . how 'bout later, okay?

MARY *kisses his cheek but doesn't wait for an answer, pushing on
ahead. Barry's not quite done yet.*

> BARRY
>
> I just think we need to do it . . . more often. Not make it so
> special. I mean, it'll be special when it happens, don't
> misunderstand me . . .

> MARY
>
> Honey, is this really the best place for that, do you think?

> BARRY
>
> Do we need vitamin C?

> MARY
>
> Uh no, we have enough. Wanna get some tissue?

Barry gets a box of Kleenex.

> BARRY
>
> I just think for right now we need to treat each other like . . .
> meat. Right? Didn't we read that? You need to see me as a
> big . . . penis. And you need to be just this huge . . . vagina.
> To me.
>> (*beat*)
> . . . It was your book.

A SOUND *escapes from Mary as she stops and turns on Barry, about to lay into him but pulling it back just in time. He looks over innocently as she shakes her head and moves off down toward the sanitary protection section.*

> BARRY

What time you gotta go to that meeting?

CUT TO:

INT. ART MUSEUM. AN EVENING THE NEXT WEEK – NIGHT

Towering marble and wood structure, broken up at intervals by frozen, overlit representations of modern art. Corinthian columns abound. TOURISTS *and* STUDENTS *wandering about.*

JERRY *makes his way along through various antechambers, looking down each passage in search of* MARY *who stands almost hidden in a distant corner, looking up at a canvas. She is turned around by Jerry and now stands dangerously close to him.*

> MARY

Hello.

> JERRY

Hi. I wasn't sure . . . you know, changing the time and all.

> MARY

No, no, I'm glad you called.

> JERRY

Yeah, I thought I'd pick somewhere a little more out of the way, you know.

> MARY

Yeah, yeah, this was a good choice.

> JERRY

You look great . . .

> MARY

Thanks. I wore the burgundy . . .

> JERRY

That's the skirt.

39

MARY

Was this okay, to meet a little bit . . . earlier?

JERRY

Yeah, absolutely. I just cancelled a seminar. It's no big thing.
God, you look . . . you just look so . . .

MARY

. . . good.
(*beat*)
I mean, it's nice that you'd do that for me.

SILENCE *between them for a moment. The beginning is always
awkward. It won't last long. He touches a hand to her cheek, then pulls
away self-consciously and looks about. She smiles.*

JERRY

So, uh . . . How's . . .?

MARY

Oh, don't ask about him . . . I mean . . . if you were going to.
You know, that's . . . that's just one thing I don't wanna . . .

JERRY

Sorry. It's just . . . he's my friend, that's all.

MARY

No, I know. I know. And I had lunch this week with . . .
(*beat*)
It doesn't mean I wanna conjure them up right now.

JERRY

You're right.
(*beat*)
It's . . .

MARY

Just . . . Could you just please . . . hold me?

JERRY

Sure.

AN EMBRACE *comes with surprising force. They kiss deeply as the shock
and lust of their first moment together overtakes them.*

40

CUT TO:

INT. HEALTH CLUB SHOWERS. A BIT AFTER THAT – DAY

A wall of mist. Barry and Cary stand alone in the steam, lazily lathering up and enjoying the warm spray of the overhead jets.

> BARRY

It's really too bad, you know?

> CARY

What?

> BARRY

I mean, I wish he'd join us. I tried his office . . . no answer.

> CARY

Why not? He only teaches a couple blocks over.
> *(beat)*
I hardly see him anymore . . . I mean, not like I used to.

> BARRY

We get together once in a while. He still calls sometimes.

> CARY

Yeah, he calls . . . but I don't see 'em that much.

> BARRY

Me neither.

> CARY

That bitch probably doesn't give him half our messages . . .
> *(beat)*
Anyhow, I think he's seeing somebody.

> BARRY

What? No.
> *(beat)*
You mean, other than his . . .?

> CARY

I guess. I mean, he's vague, you know how he is . . .

> BARRY

Oh yeah.

                         CARY

The guy's nothing if not vague. But he said something.

                         BARRY

When was this?

                         CARY

He alluded to it.

                         BARRY

Really?

                         CARY

Just a reference. But I caught it . . .

CARY *winks knowingly at Barry, who smiles in return. They stand and
turn slow circles in the water. An elbow from Cary and the two men
engage in a lazy game of shower hockey with a bar of soap, kicking it
back and forth between them.*

                         BARRY

Wow . . .

                         CARY

The guy thinks he's fucking Byron. I've always said that . . .

                         BARRY

Yes, you have. That's great . . .
                   (*beat*)
I never really liked his . . . I mean, she's nice enough, but . . .

                         CARY

Me neither. Times I met her . . .

                         BARRY

There's something . . .

                         CARY

. . . just a touch unfeminine. Is that it? Yeah, I caught it.

                         BARRY

I don't know . . . something.
                   (*beat*)
That's great. It'll get him out of his rut.

                              CARY
Yeah, maybe he'll join us.

                             BARRY
If she's young he'll have to . . .

                              CARY
Even if she's not . . . fucking 'intrigue', makes that heart
pound.

                             BARRY
Yes, it does.

THE CHATTER *stops for a moment as the two friends butt up against
one another, jockeying for position as the game nears its end. Cary
feigns right then moves left and* SLAPS *the makeshift puck loudly off
one wall. He holds his arms up victoriously as Barry smiles over at
him.*

    CUT TO:

INT. SPORTS BAR. A THURSDAY AFTERNOON – DAY

We've seen it before, only at night. A FEW WAITRESSES *move about the
mostly empty tables serving* THE SPARSE LUNCH CROWD.

THE THREE WOMEN *sit at an out-of-the-way booth, sipping coffee and
TALKING.*

                             CHERI
What?

                             TERRI
My 'ideal' fuck?

                             MARY
Yeah. Could we use some other name, please?

                             CHERI
What other name?

                             TERRI
Is there another name?

MARY

Seriously, do you mind if I record this? It's just, um . . . it's
very . . .

*The two women shrug 'No' as Mary glances about the room, taking out
a small tape recorder from her purse. She sets it up on the crisp white
linen. Cheri takes the moment to size up the joint.*

CHERI

This place is okay.

TERRI

Yeah. My boyfriend told me about it.

CHERI

I still like it . . .

Terri SNICKERS *at this while Mary* CLEARS HER THROAT *rather self-
consciously.*

BENEATH THE TABLECLOTH *Cheri tries to hold hands secretly with
Terri. Terri pulls away and places her hands on the table-top. Mary,
tape recorder in place, motions that they can begin.*

MARY

Okay, go ahead . . .

TERRI

Testing, testing . . . I just know that when I'm making love to someone . . . hey, that's what I'm there for. No matter what else is going on with us.

MARY

Right, but what about with . . .?

TERRI

Are you kidding?

MARY

You guys have been together for . . .

TERRI

Especially him! You know college professors, you gotta get a critical evaluation on everything.
(*beat*)
I'm sure he rates me on the Bell Curve . . .

The women all LAUGH OUT LOUD *at this, even Mary in spite of herself.*

See, for me, when I'm with a person . . . I figure at that moment, I am doing it because I want to be 'doing it'. I don't really want to chat, you know? And personally, I couldn't give a shit how they like the sound of my name.

MARY

But . . .

TERRI

Any talking at all, seriously, just kills it for me. Maybe it's just me, but fucking is . . . fucking. It's not a time for sharing, I don't care what anybody says.

CHERI *steals a look over at Terri, then turns back to Mary. Terri returns the look.*

45

CHERI

Yeah . . . I feel the same way.

MARY

Oh . . .

CUT TO:

INT. APARTMENT. SAME TIME – NIGHT

Jerry and Terri with their heads on their respective pillows, out of breath and staring at the ceiling.

JERRY

See? I didn't make a peep, wasn't that great? I'm really glad I raced home from rehearsal . . .
(beat)
You know, the next time you get a 'little urge' and I bust my ass getting back here in a cab, do you think you could add a little 'movement', you know, just to get the full 'Claymation' feel . . . Hey, what is the matter with you lately?

Terri turns away. Jerry tries to move closer to her without much success.

I mean, I do everything that you ask, and you're still not satisfied.

                                    TERRI
I know.

She rolls over on her stomach to escape him. Jerry is left to stare and shake his head at this newest débâcle.

CUT TO:

INT. HOTEL LOBBY. SAME TIME – DAY

Upscale hotel overlooking the lake. All ornate fabrics and vases of flowers. Straight out of Victoria *magazine and about as homey. Mary stands near Jerry, their hands secretly enfolded as* AN ASSISTANT MANAGER *works on their paperwork. They* WHISPER *to one another in quick, stolen snatches.*

                                    JERRY
Just put it on the Visa.
                          (*to Mary*)
. . . I feel optimistic, don't you?

                                    MARY
Yeah.

                                    JERRY
Why couldn't this work? Right? I mean, if we . . .
                          (*to Assistant Manager*)
You know, I just thought with the, um, you know I could just put it on the school card.
                          (*switches cards*)

                                    MARY
Yeah. I know, I know.

                                    JERRY
Everything's so tentative, I hate it, you know? . . .

                                    MARY
Me too. I do too . . .

I really . . . I do feel optimistic.

MARY

Well, I'm glad.

JERRY

You know what? You're married to him. Okay. Fine. He got
there first. I understand that. Totally. Okay? But, so what?
That's nothing, right? I mean, it's like, uh . . . um, it's not
destiny, not 'law', is it? It's just chance, really. It's no big deal.
                    (*beat*)
I see you here, with me . . . I don't know, I feel it feels like
fate.
                    (*beat*)
I just feel very, very optimistic . . .

MARY

Optimistic. Yeah.
                    (*pointing*)
I think he needs you to . . .

JERRY

Okay. You know, we don't have to do this now if you don't
want to.

MARY

Oh no, no . . . I want to. I think . . .
                    (*smiles weakly*)
Let's just not go over it so much. It just kind of makes me
feel . . .

JERRY

. . . Right.

CUT TO:

INT. HOTEL ROOM – DAY

*The straying couple. Mary puts wedding ring back on. Jerry is speaking
from the other room.*

It's never been like this. You know, never. I know that sounds
like I'm covering, 'cause this is, like, whatever . . . but this is
not me. I'm much more hard . . . firm . . . than this. I mean,
I just hope we're not blaming here, because . . .

Mary puts on her watch bracelet. Jerry enters, putting on his shirt.

I've never had this . . . Hey, do you mind looking up? Could
you just tell me, do you feel it was me?! Do you mind . . . this
is really kind of important here!! 'Cause things were . . .
everything was going very well downstairs in the lobby. I
mean, I felt really . . . I mean, is it my *imagination*? I think we
both got a little . . . Is it . . . is it me?

SILENCE *greets him and he turns away with* AN EXASPERATED
GRUNT. *He moves to his socks and shoes, pulling them on from where
he stands.*

Alright, forget it . . . It's no big deal. I mean, in essence,
we're really without sin here. It's kind of like we're Adam and
Eve in the Garden or some kind of thing. I mean, we haven't
really made a mistake yet. So . . .

THE SHOCK *of recognition between this statement and her husband's
hits Mary between the eyes. The tears begin to quietly flow.*

Look, we'll still be good friends.

MARY

Please don't . . .

JERRY

Alright. I just, you know, thought we could maybe still . . .

MARY

No.

JERRY

Come on . . .

*Jerry moves to her in a last-ditch effort. He tries to kiss her; both his
approach and her defense grow in intensity until she finally fends him
off.*

                              MARY
Just . . . just go away!! . . . Okay?

                              JERRY
Maybe we could . . .

                              MARY
Please, don't say anymore.

A NOD *from Jerry puts a cap on the discussion. He returns to his shirt and jacket hanging smartly in the closet. Mary turns to her pillow and buries her face in it.*

   CUT TO:

INT. GYM – DAY

Cary rises into frame doing sit-ups. He is listening to his headphones.

                         CARY'S VOICE
                   (*filtered through headphones*)
I feel special coming inside you. I'm serious.
                         (*whispering*)
I feel special. I'm always gonna think of you as a very special
fuck. I only hope that I can . . .

   CUT TO:

INT. ART GALLERY. SAME TIME – DAY

Inside the showroom. Barry, dressed in work duds, stands staring at the huge canvas that adorns one wall. He cocks his head from side to side, studying it. After a moment, Cheri walks over and smiles.

                              CHERI
. . . Hi.

                              BARRY
How are you?

                              CHERI
Fine, thanks.

                              BARRY
Great . . .

(*beat*)
Do you know, is this part of a collection or is it, umm . . .

CHERI
No, it's just a single piece. Nice, isn't it?

BARRY
Very.

CHERI
Your first time here?

BARRY
Uh-huh . . . you?

CHERI
No, I work here.

BARRY
Work . . . really? You're an artist?

CHERI
No. The artist's assistant.

BARRY

That's terrific.

(beat)

Hey, you don't have a gift shop, do you? I wanna buy my wife
a little . . . We're going away for the . . .

CHERI

No, I'm sorry.

BARRY

Okay. Listen, is it me, or is this whole thing sort of . . . kinda
outta whack?

THE PICTURE *is scrutinized by them both, Barry silently indicating
that it seems to lean to one side. Cheri shakes her head in disagreement.*

CHERI

No, I think it's you.

BARRY

Really? Because it seems . . .

CHERI

No, I'm sure of it. It's you.

*Barry gives her a look, then decides to take her word on it. They stand
where they are, both looking up at the massive work.*

CUT TO:

INT. HOTEL ROOM. SOME WEEKEND – NIGHT

*The same damn hotel room. A lace canopy over the four-poster bed.
Barry and Mary have retreated to opposite corners after a dismal go of
it. They are both out of breath, exhausted and frustrated. Mary glances
at her bracelet, checking the time. She lets out a little exhale of
frustration at the stopped hands, then lies back and studies the wall.*

MARY

How did you find this hotel?

BARRY

Oh, I asked around. One of the guys . . .

52

MARY

Hm.

BARRY

Maybe we should try again . . .

MARY

No. I really don't want to right now, okay?

BARRY

I'm hard, though . . . firm.
(*beat*)
If we could just relax, I'm sure we can . . .

MARY

You're whispering again.

BARRY

I'm sorry.
(*beat*)
It's okay if it's me. I don't wanna push this . . .

CUT TO:

53

INT. HOSPITAL LAB. A WEDNESDAY EARLY EVENING – DAY

Cary sitting on a stool, TALKING *on the phone while various tests run in the background. He fiddles with a model of a fetus in the mold of an anatomical womb, taking it out of the womb and tossing it like a football.*

> CARY
> Yeah . . . uh-huh. I know, yeah . . . Harvard Med? Yeah.
> That's great, top of the class too? Hm . . . AIDS research.
> Super . . . Well, hey . . . wait a minute. What the fuck's her
> name? I mean, tits like that must have a name, correct? Yeah.
> Well, you get right back to me. Okay.

CARY *hangs up the phone and sits there, holding the fetus, in both hands. Then he springs from the stool and kicks the fetus across the room, picks up his sandwich from his desk and walks out of the lab.*

CUT TO:

INT. BROWNSTONE OFFICE. SAME TIME – DAY

Cozy, sunlit nook. Fax machine and copier on an antique table. Mary struggles to hang up a framed print as the RECORDING *of the three women at lunch* PLAYS ALOUD.

> TERRI
> (*voice-over*)
> 'Maybe it's just me, but fucking is . . . fucking. It's not a time for sharing. I don't care what anyone says.'

> CHERI
> (*voice-over*)
> 'Yeah. I feel the same way.'

The tape is stopped as Mary scribbles a note to herself. She hits PLAY *again.*

> MARY
> Editorial note to delete the word 'fucking' before submitting story idea . . .
> > (*recording again*)
> '. . . not a time for sharing, I don't care what anybody says . . .'

CUT TO:

INT. HEALTH CLUB STEAM ROOM. SAME TIME – DAY

A sleekly tiled area, with benches at discreet distances from one another. White with mist. The three male friends sit in the moist heat, lying about after a workout.

> CARY
> Now, you're saying . . . what?

> BARRY
> I'm asking for 'the best' you've ever had. Can you name her?

> CARY
> 'The best . . .'

> BARRY
> Yep.

> CARY
> I mean, why do you wanna know that?

JERRY

It's interesting, no big deal.

BARRY

Come on, we're friends . . . be honest.

CARY

Well, what's your 'best', then?

BARRY

Hey, I asked the question.

CARY

Hey, fuck you, too. If we're gonna be revealing here, let's at least be fair about this stuff.

BARRY

Okay. Ahh . . . mine would be my wife.

CARY

Bullshit! Nobody'd pick their wife . . . except maybe on a talk show.

BARRY CHUCKLES *at this, elbowing Cary while Jerry watches Barry intently.*

BARRY

Yeah, well, that's my answer, and she's very good, anyway . . .
                    (*beat*)
So up yours.

CARY

Jesus . . .
                    (*beat*)
Okay, it'd be . . . the fucking 'best', huh?

BARRY

Yep.

CARY

Why do I always go first in shit like this?

BARRY

What? I just went.

56

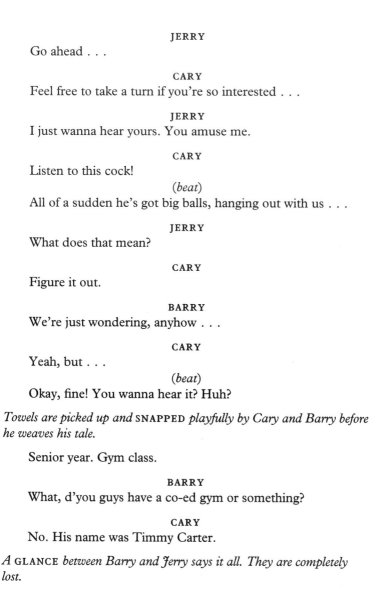

JERRY

Go ahead . . .

CARY

Feel free to take a turn if you're so interested . . .

JERRY

I just wanna hear yours. You amuse me.

CARY

Listen to this cock!
(*beat*)
All of a sudden he's got big balls, hanging out with us . . .

JERRY

What does that mean?

CARY

Figure it out.

BARRY

We're just wondering, anyhow . . .

CARY

Yeah, but . . .
(*beat*)
Okay, fine! You wanna hear it? Huh?

Towels are picked up and SNAPPED *playfully by Cary and Barry before he weaves his tale.*

Senior year. Gym class.

BARRY

What, d'you guys have a co-ed gym or something?

CARY

No. His name was Timmy Carter.

A GLANCE *between Barry and Jerry says it all. They are completely lost.*

JERRY

'Timmy'?

BARRY

Isn't that a boy's name?

CARY

He was a guy from my high school PE class . . . my best fuck.

BARRY

What?

CARY

It's the truth . . . It was almost spring vacation . . . late March
. . . and we'd had about all the shit we could take from little
Timmy. He'd turned four of us in during an English exam
earlier in the week and so . . . when the coach was down in
the lounge for a smoke, we grabbed his ass and dragged him
into the showers. We held him down, tore off his clothes . . .
and we each took a turn. I mean, we actually . . . 'did' this
guy. Up the butt! I mean, we were some crazy fuckers at that
age . . .

*A bottle of water is opened by Cary and he sucks it down while he recalls
the event.*

I was the last one. So, I don't know if he'd just given over by
this time or what, but . . . goddammit, it was . . . nice. I
mean, how can I explain this? It's never been like that with a
woman . . . as many as I fuck. Never. Never even close.
          (*beat*)
He was face down and my friends were holding him, spread
out. But Timmy and I were makin' love like we were on some
beach in the Mediterranean! I kid you not. Fuck . . . it was
amazing. I could feel him taking my rhythm. He was
clinching me off when I'd get too deep. Shit, he did
everything right! And I know he came when I did. I mean, I
didn't check or anything, but – I could tell. I shouldn't even
be telling you guys, but . . . fuck, I've never known anything
like it! Ever. Like I said, there wasn't too much of the school
year left, and Timmy dropped out . . . I guess. I mean, he
finished from home. Goddamn him. He never turned us in.
He never said a word about it to anyone. And I admired him
for that. But I think the reason he kept silent – and I feel I'm

58

right about this – is that he felt something special had happened as well. Him and me. I mean, those other guys, they just fucked him to teach him a lesson, but we . . . I know something special happened.

THE BOTTLE *is carelessly crushed by Cary as he stares off, lost in thought. He sets it down with a* TINY CLATTER *near his feet. Jerry and Barry don't make a sound. Cary smiles thinly over at his pals as Barry* CLEARS HIS THROAT, *saying nothing.*

> BARRY
>
> Jesus . . . Are you making this up?

> CARY
>
> Fuck no. This happened. I told you before, this is my life . . .

> BARRY
>
> Yeah, but . . .
>
> > (*to Jerry*)
>
> Has he told you this story?

> JERRY
>
> No. It's great though, isn't it?

> BARRY
>
> It's incredible.

> CARY
>
> You'd have taken the same steps. Common decency dictated the whole thing. I just didn't expect to find somebody who . . . you know . . . understood me, is all.
>
> > (*beat*)
>
> Anyhow, that's mine. Big deal. At least I got one.

JERRY AND BARRY *slowly shift where they are, adjusting their towels as Cary* SIGHS *and closes his eyes.*

CUT TO:

INT. HEALTH CLUB LOCKER ROOM. SAME TIME – DAY

Long rows of tediously colored metal lockers, mostly standing with their doors open. Not a soul in sight. The guys in various stages of dressing, no one talking. Cary SLAMS *his cage closed for emphasis, bare-chested and towering over his associates.*

                    CARY
By the way, you guys're crazy if you think you're out of here
without a little reciprocal . . . 'Cause I'm tired of the
sycophantic bullshit thing we got going here . . .
                    (*beat*)
. . . So, let's hear something, and I don't care who.

CARY *leans forward and studies his friends, fully expecting some
satisfaction. His friends reluctantly look back at him, fastening their
shirts and pants.*

                    BARRY
I told you mine already.

                    CARY
Fine. Bullshit, but fine.
                    (*fingers Jerry's chest*)
How about you? I think you can go ahead and climb out on a
limb, after what I just coughed up.

                    JERRY
No. I don't wanna . . .

                    CARY
What?!

                    JERRY
I'm not in the mood today. I'm late.

                    CARY
Well, fuck that, and get in the mood! You were ten minutes
ago.

                    BARRY
Right. It's your turn . . .

                    CARY
Come on. Your favorite research assistant? Fess up!

                    JERRY
Seriously, I gotta get to rehearsal.

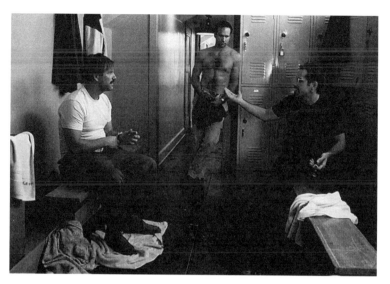

BARRY

Go ahead.

(*beat*)

I thought you said he was seeing somebody.

CARY

Oops. Come on, who is it this semester?

JERRY

Knock it off.

BARRY

Freshman or sophomore?

JERRY

What're you doing? Huh? See, this is why I hate it when the three of us get together. It just . . .

BARRY

What?

JERRY

I mean, you get together with this guy and it's like somebody slipped you an 'asshole' pill . . .

CARY

Well, we just want the truth. I thought that was the whole idea, right?

JERRY

I'm serious . . .

BARRY

What's up with you?

JERRY

Nothing, I just don't want to get into this.

AN ELBOW *from Barry digs Jerry in the ribs. He quickly finds it annoying. Jerry moves to leave but both Cary and Barry block the way.*

BARRY

Look, you're not gonna shock us, okay? I mean, not after what we just . . .

(beat)

. . . so go on.

CARY

Yeah . . . amuse us.

(beat)

And I know it's not that snatch that you live with, so don't even start in on that one.

BARRY

Exactly. Look, you can talk. It's not like you're in bed.

JERRY

What?!

BARRY

Nothing. You were the one who was complaining about it!

(to Cary)

What'd you call her the other day when we were . . .?

CARY

What? I believe it had to do with the 'feminine' issue . . .

JERRY

Fuck off! All right?

CARY

The fucking truth, then.

BARRY

Come on, we're friends. Be honest.

A JAB *to the side again from Barry sets Jerry's teeth on edge. He pulls away, looking his friends dead in the eyes.*

JERRY

Okay. The best fuck I ever had? That'd be your wife. That was the best fuck I ever had!

A QUIET *hangs over the men like the threat of rain. With a* BANG, *Jerry exits through a swinging door. Barry and Cary stand where they are, watching him go.*

CARY

That beats my story.

63

CUT TO:

INT. BROWNSTONE OFFICE. SAME TIME – DAY

Barry standing in the hallway, not moving. Mary sitting in her office, holding the receiver in one hand and staring off. Barry bends over and unties his running shoes, pulling them off along with his socks. He half tiptoes across the floor so as not to be spotted by his wife. As he passes the doorway, Mary senses his presence and turns around in her seat, quickly hanging up the phone. Barry crosses and stands behind his wife.

                            MARY
Hey.

                            BARRY
Hey.

                            MARY
You're home early.

                            BARRY
Yeah.

                            MARY
Did you guys have fun?

                            BARRY
Yeah. It was good.
                 (*beat*)
Smoking again?

                            MARY
No, just one . . .
                 (*beat*)
If you're hungry, there's . . .

                            BARRY
No, I'm fine.

                            MARY
You Okay?

                            BARRY
Yeah.

A SMILE *from her that means nothing. Not to give or receive. Barry doesn't return it but wanders off toward the staircase. Mary returns to her work.*

CUT TO:

INT. APARTMENT. A WEEK OR SO LATER – DAY

Terri home after work but still hard at it. Another ad campaign in a pile on a nearby table, with reference books scattered about as SEVERAL MORE BOOKS *are pulled down from various shelves in Terri's quest for a Webster's.*

> TERRI
>
> Shit!

CAMUS *tumbles to the floor along with one or two other volumes. Terri hurriedly scoops them up as* A PERFUMED SCRAP OF PAPER *tumbles free of the dust cover. Curious, she picks it up. Terri studies the number and then sniffs the page. It seems familiar but the memory doesn't come. She brings Camus and the bit of stationery to the couch with her as she continues to smell the paper and turn it over in her hands.*

> (reading)
>
> 'Hold me . . .'?

CUT TO:

INT. APARTMENT. A TOUCH LATER – DAY

Terri sitting on the couch, still staring at the paper. The impression of scarlet lips. She's pulled the phone a little closer, but hasn't committed yet. TERRI *shakes her head at these new-found feelings of jealousy, smiling weakly to herself as she hurriedly lies down on the bed and dials the number.*

> TERRI
>
> Is this your work phone? Oh, your little office there? Yeah, right. I remember it. Great. I just had it written down here with something else. Right. Maybe you gave it over lunch. I . . . I don't remember.

(*beat*)

Anyway, you're good? Terrific. Listen, like I said, I kind of just called by accident, but you want to get salads or something?

CUT TO:

INT. APARTMENT — LATER

Terri is on the floor tearing pages out of the book.

CUT TO:

INT. ART GALLERY. DAYS LATER — DAY

The office area is overstuffed with mail, canvasses wrapped in brown paper and clutter. A dusty clock stares down at Cheri, who gives it another glance as she dials A HANDHELD PHONE *repeatedly, pushing the numbers in an endless cycle.*

> CHERI
> . . . answer.
> > (*tries again*)
> Answer . . .
> > (*tries again*)
> Answer . . .
> > (*tries again*)
> Answer . . .

CUT TO:

INT. STUDIO. SAME TIME — NIGHT

Tiny bathroom. Black and white everything. A WOMAN *sits hunched on the toilet in one corner, head in her hands. Cary is heard prowling outside the door. A sliver of light near the jam.*

> CARY
> You're a tramp, are you aware of that? A prick-fucking teaser, and I don't mind saying it to your face! If you'd come out of there, I'd say it right in your fucking face! Oh, God. You lied to me, right to my own fucking person. I'm serious, you are not a nice woman . . .

(beat)
I mean, who in the fuck just gets their period all of a sudden?
Huh?! It just doesn't just happen – I mean, and it's happened
all over my bedding! But, no, you knew that and you're
twisted to have planned this.
(beat)
I hope to God you've got one of those red biohazard bags in
your purse, 'cause you just bought yourself a set of linens!
Three hundred and eighty thread count! Bullshit!

A DESPERATE PULL *on the door as Cary jerks the knob violently from
the hallway. It doesn't give.*

What's the matter!
(listens)
You feeling sick? Huh?! Crampy? How 'bout this: try shoving
two aspirins up your crack and never, ever, fucking call me in
the morning! Got that?! That's my own remedy . . .
(beat)
Now, I'm going down to grab a beer and I guess some fuckin'
409! Be gone when I get back. 'Kay?

A DOOR SLAMS *in the distance. The woman stays where she is, head
bowed.*

CUT TO:

INT. LOFT. SAME TIME – NIGHT

*Cheri's futon couch has been pulled out into a bed and she and Terri lie
beneath brightly colored blankets in a peaceful silence. A radio softly
plays* COOL JAZZ *somewhere in the room.*

> CHERI
God. That was . . .

> TERRI
Mmm-hmmm.

> CHERI
You're just . . . that's all I can say.

TERRI *smiles lazily over at her, closing her eyes. Cheri waits.*

67

. . . and?

                         TERRI
'And?'
                        (*beat*)
I mean, do I really have to say it? You couldn't tell?

                         CHERI
No, I could. I think I could. I wanted to. . .

                         TERRI
Hear it? Okay . . . I loved it.
                        (*beat*)
I did.

CHERI *snuggles closer, invading Terri's space a bit.*

                         CHERI
Thank you. What did you like best?

                         TERRI
Oh Jesus. . .

                         CHERI
No, just so I'll remember. . .

                         TERRI
You don't have to . . . listen, I'm not gonna want our
'Greatest Hits' from now on . . . so, do whatever. Okay?

                         CHERI
But just one . . . like one thing. Only one thing. Just tell
me . . .

                         TERRI
Shit.
                        (*beat*)
Okay, you know what I like? The silence. When we were
making love, you were quiet. I liked that.

A KISS *to her partner's forehead and Terri turns away, basking in the
quiet of the tiny room.*

CUT TO:

INT. APARTMENT. SAME TIME – NIGHT

Jerry in his briefs, watching TV in an unearthly blue light. After a moment, Terri comes heavily into the room and immediately starts to undress.

> JERRY
>
> Happened to you?
>
> (*beat*)
>
> We ran late. . .

Terri LAUGHS OUT LOUD *at this one.*

> I was gonna . . . I tried your pager, but there wasn't any, uh. . .
>
> (*beat*)
>
> I even buzzed you here.

A SMIRK *as she holds up the answering machine for Jerry's inspection. The light isn't flashing.*

> TERRI
>
> Really?

> JERRY
>
> I didn't leave a message on the machine. I . . . I hung up before the . . .

TERRI *waves him off as she moves toward the bathroom. Jerry watches her undress a moment, then turns back to the TV.*

> CUT TO:

INT. COFFEE SHOP – DAY

Quiet today. A FEW PATRONS *eating in far-off corners. Light spills in from a series of greasy windows.*

BARRY AND CARY *sit in a booth, enjoying a lunch of coney dogs after a workout.*

> BARRY
>
> Do you think you're good?

CARY

What, a good fuck?

BARRY

No, 'good'. I'm asking you, do you think you're good?

CARY

'Good', what do you mean, 'good'? What kinda question is that?

BARRY

I'm asking . . . I'm saying are you, you know, like, a 'good person'?

CARY

Hey, I'm eating lunch. . .

BARRY

So?

CARY

So, why'd you invite me here, to ask if I'm good or not?

BARRY

I just . . .

CARY

'Good' . . .
(smiles)
Right? This girl tried to dump me once. So, I got my hands on some hospital stationery, and I sent her this letter informing her that her name had appeared on a list of previous partners of a patient of mine who had just tested HIV positive . . .

BARRY

You did not do that.

CARY

Oh yeah.
(beat)
So, you decide. The bitch deserved it – she never understood me – it was a good joke, but am I 'good' for doing it? Fuck if I know. All I know's I did it, and I find a certain clarity in the gesture.

But don't you think we're gonna have to . . . I mean, like pay
for all this in the end?

CARY

Possibly. I mean, if there ends up being a God or something
like that whole eternity thing out there, like, then, yeah,
probably so. I dunno. We'll see. But until then, we're on my
time, okay? The interim is mine.

BARRY

Okay, fine, I'll put it another way. Take . . . me.

CARY

Oh Christ, come on . . .

BARRY

No, who better I should ask? We're friends, you're around
me, so . . . I'm asking.

CARY

Fine . . . I think you're a marvelous human being. I mean it.
Now shut up and eat.

BARRY

Come on, I'm serious here. . . .
                    (beat)
It's no big deal. I'm just talking. I've just been thinking a lot
lately.

CARY

I bet . . .
                    (beat)
You say anything to her about it yet?

BARRY

No. I tried a million times, but she . . .

THE CHILI DOGS take a few more hits as the men mull over the
universe.

So, I mean, if you didn't know me, I mean, at all . . .

CARY

Oh Jesus!

BARRY

No, seriously, you would still feel that way?

CARY

Knock it off . . . what is this?!

BARRY

Nothing . . . I'm just . . .

CARY

See, man . . . you go around like this all day, I'd cheat on you, too.
(*beat*)
Sorry, fuck . . . that wasn't nice.

BARRY

That's okay. I know you didn't mean it.

CARY

Forget about it, man. It's the best thing, I promise you . . .

BARRY

Yeah.
(*beat*)
Anyway, I was just wondering.

CARY

Yeah, but that's not something you should be doing. That's something for our little thespian friend to think about.

BARRY

I'm gonna talk to him. Seriously . . .

CARY

It's that girlfriend of his.

BARRY

Yeah, what are you gonna do?

CARY

I think I still got some of that stationery.

Barry laughs.

Kidding.

CUT TO:

INT. BOOK STORE – DAY

Ma & Pa's place, this time in a back section. Endless rows to the ceiling. Musty and almost frightening, but filled with bargains. Cary is cruising some 'Mark Down' bins when he spots A WOMAN *with her back to him. Long and lean and reading a book; that's all the introduction he needs. He bides his time until* A MOLDY VOLUME *slips from her fingers and hits the floor. He is instantly there with a smile and helping hand. They stare at one another with a hazy sense of recognition. It is Terri.*

> CARY
>
> Afternoon.

> TERRI
>
> Hi.

> CARY
>
> Anything good?

> TERRI
>
> Depends. Can you read?

> CARY
> (*chuckles*)
> Actually, I came over because . . . aren't you . . .?

> TERRI
>
> Yeah, I thought I recognized you. How are you?

> CARY
>
> I'm great.

> TERRI
>
> That's nice.

THEIR HANDS *quickly meet in a handshake, followed by a smile.*

CARY

You? How're you doing?

TERRI

Well, couldn't be better.
            (*she chuckles*)

CARY

Well, that's good to hear. You're looking for a bargain?

TERRI

Yeah. Actually, I stopped in because I got a tip from . . .

CARY

Isn't that funny? Well, so did I. Well, I heard him talking about it, anyway. Small world . . .

TERRI

Oh. That is funny . . .

CARY

I half expected to find him here.

TERRI

So . . .

                         CARY

Yeah, so, so, so . . . This is odd, isn't it? Just running into
anyone you know in a city this size.

                         TERRI

Oh, yeah.

                         CARY

Like fate.

                         TERRI

Oh God, not 'fate'.

                         CARY

Why?

                         TERRI

Sorry, I just hear that word thrown about our place a lot.
So . . .

                         CARY

He loves those Greeks, doesn't he?

                         TERRI

Yeah. Anyway . . .

                         CARY

Yeah, anyway . . .
                        (*beat*)
You wanna get some coffee?

                         TERRI

Umm . . .
                (*looking around nervously*)
Actually, I'm waiting for someone.

                         CARY

Okay. What about later? I'd even go for decaf . . .

                         TERRI

Ahh, no. No, thank you, though.
                        (*beat*)
I have . . .

CARY

Why not? Huh?

A CUSTOMER *drifts past and Terri looks about self-consciously.*

TERRI

Do you . . .? What are you doing? Why are you acting
like . . .

CARY

Because I want to take you out. It's just coffee. Don't say
'No' . . .

TERRI

Well, I already did. I could say it again for you. 'No'. Leave
me alone.

*Cary moves closer now, like a shark spotting a swimmer off Miami
Beach. His teeth flash a wicked smile. MacHeath and then some.*

CARY

Okay, I see . . .
                              (*beat*)
You're a real piece 'a work, you know that?

TERRI

That's great.

CARY

Nobody actually *likes* you. You're aware of this, right?

TERRI

Are you for real?

CARY

I don't get your kind. You give my friend nothing but grief
. . . always coming off like some dyke bitch. How do you live
with yourself?!

TERRI

What the fuck is the matter with you?!!

CARY

Hey! You don't want to have a drink with me, that's fine. I

can take it. I have a healthy self image. But you keep dicking people I know . . . one of these days, I'm gonna find you and I'm gonna knock you on your ass!!

THE BOOK *that he had picked up for Terri earlier is now tossed to the floor again. It* SLAPS *against the wood with a* BANG!

You are a useless cunt. Get used to it.

CARY *butts his face to hers and then turns and* SMASHES *out of the place, the door* ROCKING *on its hinges. A* FEW READERS *look up. Terri stands frozen, unable even to pick up the bargain volume that lies on the floor.*

CUT TO:

INT. SUPERMARKET — NIGHT

A modern chain-store shoved into the bottom of a high-rise. A FEW SHOPPERS *and* STORE CREW MEMBERS *bustling about in their shiny red vests. Terri and Cheri moving about the aisles, picking up a few items for a quick dinner. Cheri carries a hand basket and tags after Terri like a small dog.*

TERRI

It's just a shitty day.

CHERI

Fine.

Cheri is about to speak, thinks better of it, and picks up a box of Tampax Supers while Terri checks her watch.

Oh, this is great.
(*reading*)
Did you write this?

TERRI

That's cute.

CHERI

It's really good.

TERRI

Ohh. Anyhow, Mondays are still okay. Alright?

CHERI

Monday's still good?

TERRI

Yes.

CHERI

No, 'cause I told you I could change my stuff around, if you . . .

TERRI

I said 'Yes'. He's got that class . . . you know, he usually goes late.

CHERI

But what if he doesn't . . .?
                    (*beat*)
Why can't you just tell him?

TERRI

Because I like the fact that he thinks he's the only one who's fucking around. I enjoy it.

CHERI

Oh, great. I'm glad I can be of some service.

TERRI

That's not what I meant.

CHERI

Just tell me why . . .?

TERRI

Please don't. Don't question everything, okay? You're very tiring . . .

A CHECKSTAND *is finally reached and they shuffle into it, trying to* TALK QUIETLY *amidst their fellow shoppers.*

Look, I love you. Okay? Huh?

CHERI

I know.

TERRI

I do, I do, but your questions are so . . . useless. You know?

CHERI

I know . . . I do know, you know.

TERRI

But you ask so fucking many of them. I mean, I love being
with you. I've said that. This is not a barometer reading I'm
giving you here. It lasts.

CHERI

I know.

TERRI

Okay? So, you have to believe me.

CHERI

I do.

TERRI

No, you don't. You don't or you wouldn't waste our time
wandering around a grocery store asking me about the degree
to which I like being with you . . .
(beat)
I can't explain it better than that, but you just . . .

CHERI

I'm sorry.

TERRI

Don't be sorry. You didn't do anything. You just . . . you just
talk too much. Jesus.

*Terri moves forward in line; Cheri picks up a magazine and follows her
a minute later.*

INT. ART MUSEUM. ONE AFTERNOON – DAY

*Mary wandering on her own. After a moment, Jerry approaches from
the opposite direction, a bag from a bookstore swinging in one hand as
he leads* A HANDFUL OF STUDENTS *about (including* THE YOUNG
WOMAN *from the earlier class).*

JERRY

. . . They were, in fact, young boys, and it wasn't until the

Restoration that women appeared on stage, but in reality many of them were prostitutes, which was . . .

Jerry stops cold when he sees Mary and remains there until she catches sight of him. He motions for his class to go on ahead.

Listen, why don't you guys head on in to the Age of Reason, okay? I'll catch up with you. I gotta make a phone call. Just right over there, by the Voltaire statue.

Jerry walks up to Mary.

JERRY

Hi.

MARY

Hello.

JERRY

Wow, this is . . . this is . . . Um . . . Look, I'm sorry I haven't called you. Actually, I tried to, but then I lost the office number and, uh God, this is weird, isn't it? Um, I'm just here with a bunch of kids doing some research, but . . .

MARY

Yeah, she's cute.

JERRY

No, no, they're students. What?

Jerry sits beside Mary.

Hey, could we . . . do you think we could talk maybe, just get together . . .?

Mary gathers up her things and walks away from Jerry.

MARY

No.

Jerry follows her.

JERRY

Look, can we just stop and maybe . . . Come here.

Mary stops and turns toward Jerry.

Whoa! I'd like to try to at least . . .

Please . . . please leave me alone.

I need to talk, at least get some closure, or . . .

What you need is the last thing on Earth that I'm interested in, alright?

(*beat*)

The same hotel room? I mean, the exact same . . .

Yes, that was . . . I just suggested it to him. He asked me, and then . . .

How could you do that?

I don't know.

How?!

I was jealous, okay? I guess I just, I mean . . . I wanted to be there first. I wanted to feel that . . .

Well, you weren't. You never were . . .

I know, but I wanted to pretend like I was. You know . . .

Why?

Because I just . . . I felt . . .

(*shrugs*)

MARY

I didn't want it to be the same thing. That's the only reason I agreed to do it in the first . . . I wanted it to be different. That's the only way I wanted to do it, if somehow it'd be different . . .

JERRY

Okay, that's fine. I understand. That's fair. But . . . I mean, we're here now, aren't we? Aren't we? The two of us. I mean, that's gotta like, be something, you know. Fate, or . . .

MARY

Actually, I'm here doing a feature for . . .

JERRY

Yeah, but, I mean, how many times a year do you actually come here? I mean, I'm hardly ever . . .
                    (sees it isn't working)
I mean, this is . . . shit. It's just so . . . How did things ever get so . . .?

MARY

Because life is complicated. People can't communicate. And you couldn't keep your erection . . .

JERRY

I know, but that's never . . .

MARY

It's just one big cycle for me.

JERRY

I keep thinking about this and we just can't end like this.

MARY

Goodbye.

JERRY

Could we please?

Mary turns on her heel and walks away. Jerry is left standing there, unable to do anything but watch her go.

CUT TO:

An austere room, although still not completely decorated. Dinner set for two. Barry and Mary eating across from each other at one end of a long table. Candles flicker.

BARRY

. . . so, what do you think? Honey?

MARY

What?

BARRY

About seeing them again. Wouldn't that be nice?

MARY

Mmm-hmm . . .

BARRY

No?

MARY

I mean, yeah, if you want to . . . yeah.

BARRY

Doesn't sound like you do.

MARY

Well, to be honest, I'd just like to get the house done a bit more.

BARRY

Right . . .

MARY

Haven't finished much since the last time they were here.

BARRY

Well, we could all go out then, maybe.

MARY

Okay . . .

BARRY

What's the matter?

MARY

Nothing.

BARRY

You seem nervous.

MARY

Why would I be . . .?

BARRY

I dunno.

MARY

Well, I'm not! I'm . . . fine.

BARRY

Yeah, I mean, why would you be nervous about seeing them?
I don't know. Why?

She studies her husband.

MARY

Honey, what is this?

BARRY

Nothing.

MARY

What're you doing?!

BARRY

Not a thing . . .
(*beat*)
You? What've you been doing?

MARY
(*it all falls away*)
What do you mean? I've been, working on the house, I'm
trying to, and I've been writing my . . . I don't know what you
mean, 'doing', I made dinner and . . . I . . .
(*beat*)
What did he say to you?

BARRY

You tell me. Why don't you tell me what he said to me? I've

84

been waiting to see if you'd do something about it, but . . .
(*beat*)
So, is it true?

Silence.

Mary nods.

Huh, I figured it was, but, you know . . . benefit of the doubt.

MARY
What do you want me to say?

BARRY
Nothing. No, that pretty much says it all . . .
(*beat*)
It's good bread.

A fork is dropped with a CLATTER *as Barry gathers himself up.*

He rises and disappears down the hallway. She sits back and tries to take in some air. Huge gulps but it doesn't seem to help.

CUT TO:

INT. BROWNSTONE LIVING ROOM. ANOTHER TIME – DAY

Bare as the day they moved in. Boxes stacked in corners. Picture frames leaning against the wall. Mary enters from the kitchen with an armful of dishes and tucks them into a waiting carton. She tapes it closed, looks around briefly and exits.

CUT TO:

INT. THE THEATER. A MONTH OR SO LATER – DAY

Actors are on stage in costume for a dress rehearsal.

Barry is standing in the aisle between rows of empty seats.

Jerry is onstage in costume and make-up giving direction to the young actress.

JERRY
And use the fan more! Because it's all behind the eyes, you really had it in the monologue the other day . . .

As Jerry looks out into the audience, Barry waves. Jerry excuses himself from the young actress.

> You know what? I'm gonna talk to him for a second. Why don't you just go hang out in the greenroom for about fifteen minutes. Okay? I'll be there.

The young actress walks offstage as Jerry walks down into the auditorium to meet Barry.

JERRY

Hey.

BARRY

Hey. Sorry to interrupt and all but . . . you never returned my messages, so . . .

(*beat*)

Show looks good.

JERRY

No, it's all right. Just a dress rehearsal . . . but thanks. It's Wycherley.

Barry shrugs.

> Doesn't matter . . . Look, I'm sorry . . . I mean . . .

BARRY

Forget it. That's not why I came here.

JERRY

No, I should've come to you.

BARRY

Why? I would've said 'No'.

JERRY

I . . . I don't mean in the beginning. I just meant I should talk . . . It was a shitty thing to let happen in the first place. I just feel . . . fuck, I don't know how to put this, I just feel . . .

BARRY

'Bad'?

                    JERRY

'Bad'. Exactly! Bad.

                    BARRY

I mean, my wife . . .

                    JERRY

I'm sorry.

                    BARRY

The same hotel room even.

                    JERRY

I am sorry.

                    BARRY

Yeah . . .

                    JERRY

But I . . . I mean, I still feel . . .

                    BARRY

. . . 'bad'.

                    JERRY

Right. 'Bad'.
                    (*beat*)
So, are you guys talking at all?

                    BARRY

No. I don't even know where she's . . . I mean, she'll call.

                    JERRY

Oh yeah. They always call.

                    BARRY

Has . . . has she called you?

                    JERRY

Me? No! God no!

                    BARRY ·

Right.

                    JERRY

I just meant they . . .

                         BARRY
Right.

CUT TO:

INT. STUDIO – SAME TIME

Cary sits shirtless and wrapped in sheets in the middle of his love nest. He talks toward a closed bathroom doorway across the room.

                         CARY
                       (*to himself*)
What, are you borrowing toiletries in there?! No? Yes? What the fuck.
                       (*beat*)
So, look, I know you're nervous and all, so it's . . . But if you use any towels in there – and please don't feel like . . . I always do this . . . it's a health thing, strictly, I mean, really it is – Take a shower if you want to. Wipe yourself off, no problem. But set anything you do use off to one side. Okay? I gotta do a wash, anyway. Okay?

CUT TO:

INT. ART GALLERY. SOME EVENING LATER ON – NIGHT

The main gallery. Jerry wanders about, taking in the room and its art but with an eye out for Cheri. He stops for a moment in front of the large hanging canvas and, without meaning to, studies it. After a moment Cheri, dressed in a sweater, mini and Docs, moves to him and smiles.

                         CHERI
Hi.

                         JERRY
How're you?

                         CHERI
Fine, thanks.

JERRY

Great . . .

(*beat*)

Do you know, is this part of a collection, or is it, uh . . .

CHERI

No, that's just a single piece. Nice, isn't it?

JERRY

Very, very.

CHERI

Yeah. First time here?

JERRY

Mm-hm. You?

CHERI

No, I work here.

JERRY

Oh, really . . . Work? Are you an artist, or . . .?

CHERI

No, I'm the artist's assistant.

JERRY

Oh, an 'assistant'. Huh? Wow . . .

CHERI

Is there anything I can help you with, or . . .?

JERRY

Look, I'm . . . I'm . . . I'm the guy that she lives with. I just
. . . I just thought I'd introduce myself, or . . . you know . . .

CHERI

Who?

JERRY

Come on . . .

(*beat*)

She told me that the two of you were together . . . or
whatever . . . It's just . . .

CHERI

That's what I thought. Well, look, um, there's really nothing else I can show you here, then . . . I mean, if you're done looking. Right?

JERRY

You know, you could show me why she'd be interested in somebody like you.

CHERI

Maybe because I don't say stupid fucking things like that to people.
(*phone rings*)
I got a call . . .

JERRY

Great . . .
(*studying the canvas*)
Your painting's crooked.

CUT TO:

INT. COFFEE SHOP. ANOTHER TIME – DAY

The old stomping grounds, dead quiet on a weekend afternoon. A FEW CUSTOMERS ABOUT *as* TERRI AND JERRY *finish a meal at a secluded booth.*

JERRY

I just feel . . . I don't know. But I want to say this, I need to . . . listen . . . we both . . . all this – what I've done as well – there have been some mistakes. Okay?

TERRI

Fine.

JERRY

You know, I mean, 'cause you've done the same . . . this whole 'girl' thing is . . .

TERRI

I said 'Fine'. That's how you feel. Fine . . .

JERRY

But . . . you aren't coming back, right? I mean . . . what,
that's it? This whole thing we've had, it's just over?

TERRI

Look, I know about her. You know that, right? What
happened . . . I mean, how you two had your little . . .
(*beat*)
Listen, let's just leave it there, because . . .

JERRY

Don't you think I feel . . .

TERRI

What, 'bad'?

JERRY

Of course I do. The guy's practically my best friend.

TERRI

Oh, don't even fucking use that, alright? 'Best friend'? That is
bullshit. Try saying 'friend' when you're down there lapping
between his wife's legs. See how it sounds then.

JERRY

Come on, alright? It was a mistake. I know . . .

TERRI

Why are we doing this? I never thought this arrangement
would be . . . What do you want? Huh? We had something
nice. We paid the bills . . . great. But now it's . . .

JERRY

Look, if you knew, why didn't you tell me? We could've . . .
maybe we could've talked about it, or . . .

TERRI

Look, you started seeing somebody, it doesn't matter. I met
someone, too – I mean, I at least tried to fuck outside our
calling circle, but, hey – if we could've come back together
and continued, then it would've been very sweet. But we
can't. We fucked it. We fucked up . . .

JERRY

You know what? No, it doesn't have to be like that.

TERRI

Hey, it's just all . . . very fucked.
>> (*beat*)

Wake up!

JERRY

No, it doesn't have to be . . .

TERRI

Wake up! Wake up!

JERRY

Hey! Hey . . . hey . . . shhh! Would you just fuckin' listen to me for a second!
>> (*beat*)

Every time I try to . . . I'm trying to apologize or whatever, and you just keep fuckin' whacking me down! I feel like I'm . . .

TERRI

Listen, I don't have time. Okay? It's late! So, let's just do this. It's over. Thanks so much, it was lovely. I'll get the rest of my stuff later.
>> (*beat*)

Lunch was a mistake . . .

A sandwich drops back on to her plate and Terri starts to stand. Jerry catches a wrist and holds on.

She pulls away but stays seated as he RAMBLES ON. A COUPLE *nearby hurries and finishes their meal to get out of the crossfire.*

JERRY

This is just . . . so . . . shitty! I mean, after all . . .

TERRI

God, please don't fucking examine . . . You are so weird about shit like this! You just wanna turn it all over and over in your . . . This is not some fucking thesis, okay, so snap out of it!

JERRY

(*whispers*)

Would you please be quiet.

TERRI

That's my advice to you . . . Grow the fuck up.

JERRY

This is . . .

(*beat*)

Okay, can I like . . . do I . . . at least get a number? You know, if you get mail or something?

A BOOK *near Jerry's elbow is hurriedly turned over and a number scribbled inside its cover. She hands it over.*

TERRI

Sure. Should I, um, write 'Hold me' or anything like that?

JERRY

That's not funny.

TERRI

Yes, it is.

Terri smiles once and stands after dropping a dollar on to the table. Terri doesn't get far before Jerry stands and SPEAKS, *bringing unwanted eyes to their conversation. She flinches at this but holds her ground.*

JERRY

So . . . are you . . .? I mean, so you're staying with her now?

TERRI

God, not her too . . .

JERRY

No, 'cause I just can't . . .

TERRI

Can't what?! Why do you find it so hard to fathom that I'd want to be with a woman? I mean, I wanted to be with you . . . now I want to be with her. That's all.

                              JERRY
I know, it just makes me feel a little, you know . . . Oh fuck!
Alright, great! Just forget it!

                              TERRI
I mean, is this a moral issue . . . or is it just because you think
I have nice tits?

A REPLY *is lost on her as she walks out the* EXIT. *He stands near his
table, oblivious to the uncomfortable glances nearby.*

                              JERRY
It's both.

CUT TO:

INT. APARTMENT. ONE NIGHT – NIGHT

Jerry's place, inside the bathroom. WE *can just make the man himself
out in the distance in passionate embrace with* THE YOUNG ACTRESS
from his play. They GIGGLE *as he pulls her to the bed and she pretends
to resist.*

*Jerry suddenly stops for a moment, pulling away. He discreetly snags a
hand phone from the coffee table.*

                              JERRY
Are you Okay? Do you want anything?

*The Young Actress just lays there. Jerry moves to the bathroom. Sitting
on the toilet, Jerry begins dialing a number. He lets it* RING FOR SHORT
BURSTS, *then hangs up, dials the number again over and over.*

Answer.
                             (*beat*)
Answer . . .

CUT TO:

INT. LOFT. SAME TIME – NIGHT

*Terri sitting up in the futon bed, aimlessly flipping through cable
channels. Cheri slumps near her legs, kissing them and trying to get her
partner interested. It isn't working. The* PHONE RINGS IN SHORT,
LOUD BURSTS *periodically throughout. No one answers it.*

CHERI

Answer . . . answer me.

(beat)

Look, this is not just another question. I . . . I . . . Please
answer me . . . please.

*Infomercials continue to get flicked through as Terri stares at the visuals,
never acknowledging her partner.*

CUT TO:

INT. BROWNSTONE BEDROOM. SAME TIME – NIGHT

*Barry lies deep under the comforter, masturbating in the near darkness
while on the phone. He goes along in silence for a moment but he is not
reaching climax.*

BARRY

What's your name? Yeah, oh yeah, that's nice. That's pretty.
That's . . .

(to himself)

What's going on?

(into phone)

Listen, I gotta go. No, it's not . . .

*He hangs up as more attempts are made but with the same results.
Barry lies in the empty bed, CALLING OUT into the darkness. There is
no answer.*

Come on! Shit! What is the matter! Oh God, is it me?

(he tries again)

Is it me?

CUT TO:

INT. STUDIO. SAME TIME – NIGHT

*Cary sits up in the middle of his bed, talking to A WOMAN who lies
turned away from him. She remains perfectly still in the black puddle of
his bedding as he SPEAKS to her.*

CARY

I put it in you, you cry. I stick it down by your ass, you cry –

which is fair, I grant you, that hurts, but – I kiss your tits, I touch you or so much as fucking rub up against you . . . and you're weeping in my pillow! Is it me . . . I don't think so!!

She is turned over gently by Cary and pulled close to him. Her eyes seem red and raw. It is Mary.

Alright?

> MARY
>
> Can . . . can you just . . . just hold me.

> CARY
>
> I want to make love . . .
> *(pats her stomach)*
> A few more months it's not gonna be so easy, you know.

> MARY
>
> Uh-huh.
> *(beat)*
> We will. Just a few minutes . . .

> CARY
>
> But we will fuck tonight, right?

> MARY
>
> Yes. In a minute . . .

AN ARM *is thrown carelessly around her shoulders, pulling her near. She closes her eyes and melts back into the contact. Cary steals a glance at her wrist for the time. He frowns as he studies the watch.*

> CARY
>
> Jesus . . . your fucking watch doesn't even work!

> MARY
>
> No, that's . . .

> CARY
> *(pulling it off her arm)*
> I'll get you another one . . .
> *(beat)*
> Jesus, you're a mess. Lay back.

THE WATCH *is unceremoniously tossed on a black nightstand by Cary as Mary makes a limp grab for it. She just misses it. She stares at it while Cary pulls her to him and rubs her breasts.*

How's that feel?

MARY

That's nice.

SLOW FADE OUT TO:

SILENCE. DARKNESS.